To the North Pole

by Bronwyn Miller
illustrated by Ron Himler

Practice Decodable 65

McGraw Hill Education

Bothell, WA • Chicago, IL • Columbus, OH • New York, NY

MHEonline.com

Send all inquiries to:
McGraw-Hill Education
8787 Orion Place
Columbus, OH 43240

ISBN: 978-0-02-145045-9
MHID: 0-02-145045-5

Printed in China.

8 9 10 11 12 DSS 27 26 25 24 23

Long ago, explorers had a goal.
Explorers hoped to find the North Pole.

In 1908, a boat came to a frozen coast.

It sat in ice and snow.

Brave explorers left the boat.
They traveled in blowing snow.

Men in heavy coats drove sleds.
The sleds were loaded with supplies.
Supplies did grow low.

There were no roads to follow.

No arrows showed the way.

Some men turned back.

Some men kept going.
These brave explorers reached their goal.
They did find the North Pole!